IMAGES OF ENGLAND

CHESHAM

IMAGES OF ENGLAND

CHESHAM

COLIN J. SEABRIGHT

TEMPUS

Frontispiece: The Market Hall, often called the Town Hall, is pictured here around 1920. This scene was instantly recognizable as Chesham but is now only a memory since it was demolished in 1965 to ease traffic flow.

First published 2004

Tempus Publishing Limited
The Mill, Brimscombe Port,
Stroud, Gloucestershire, GL5 2QC
www.tempus-publishing.com

British Library Cataloguing in Publication Data.
A catalogue record for this book is available from the British Library.

ISBN 0 7524 3367 9

Typesetting and origination by Tempus Publishing Limited.
Printed in Great Britain.

Contents

This light-hearted postcard was produced by William Butts who was Chesham's most prolific photographer at the end of the nineteenth century and in the early years of the twentieth. The original caption with this postcard read, 'Please policeman, though he's not muzzled, he's under control'.

Acknowledgements

The majority of the pictures are based on postcards and photographs in my own collection but I gratefully acknowledge the assistance of Mr Adrian Kerwood, the former director of the Chesham Town Museum Project, who lent items from their collection of rare photographs identified (CTMP) at the end of the accompanying texts. I must also express my gratitude to William Butts, Sydney Jowett and all the other anonymous local photographers whose work is featured here. I sincerely apologize if I have unwittingly infringed copyright on any of these pictures but I believe all such rights to have expired.

Introduction

Chesham, a small Buckinghamshire market town, sits in a narrow valley in the
Chiltern Hills, the source of the River Chess. The restricted width of level ground
between the hillsides forced the town to develop along the valley and, with a total built-
up length of 3 miles including Waterside and Newtown, it was once claimed to be the
longest town in the country for its size.

The first documented evidence of the town is in AD 970 but the site was occupied
several centuries earlier when repeated ploughing by Saxon farmers created The Balks
across the slope of the hill. The Market was established in 1257 and Chesham became
the focus for the surrounding villages. In the sixteenth century, most of Chesham's
workers were employed in the leather and clothing trades and others as wheelwrights,
mostly individual craftsmen working from home. Later craft industries included straw-
plaiting, chair bodging and general turnery.

In 1822 travel writer William Cobbett described Chesham as 'a nice little town, lying
in a deep and narrow valley, with a stream of water running through it'. A few years
later, a guide described the country around Chesham as 'beautifully diversified and very
picturesque, famous for the growth of the beech tree, from which articles are made,
such as malt-shovels, brush-blocks hoops in all sizes, and bowls, etc'. In Victoria's reign,
Chesham became a town of small industries still based on craftmanship. Some of the old
workshops disappeared, others grew into small factories, boot manufacturers began to
export, and steam power was introduced into the mills.

In 1898 a county guide comments 'Chesham is a bustling little town, nestling between
the spurs of two lofty hills, up whose sides it has already thrown a few tentative streets.
The countryside is charmingly diversified, a noticeable feature being the great number
of beech trees, which, however, are gradually disappearing for commercial purposes.'

A 1903 town guide contains this description: 'Chesham is reached from London by
the Metropolitan Railway and lies in a basin almost surrounded by spurs of the Chiltern
Hills. The town is situated in a district celebrated for its beautiful woodland, green
pastures and pleasant glades. The advent of the railway has in recent years somewhat
changed the aspect of the town itself, many of its quaint gables having given place to
modern shop-fronts. Chesham is neither sleepy nor idle. The town is a veritable hive of
industry. The visitor has only to pass up the main street at the time of the midday meal
to fully realize this fact. Today, as in the old days, the town is famous for its boots and
shoes, and thousands of brushes are made and dispatched to colonial and foreign markets.
Here, too, is manufactured almost every kind of woodenware from the simple hoop and
toy spade to the delicately carved butter print and bread plate. Watercress is grown in
considerable quantities and large numbers of Aylesbury ducks are reared in the locality'.

In 1930 another guide noted that, 'There is no other market town within a radius
of 30 miles of London, possessing so much of the picturesque, combined with business
energy, as Chesham. The town is, of necessity, being enlarged; it is stretching out its

borders towards the hills where modern villas are springing up. Chesham is well-favoured with respect for the variety of its occupations', but author S.P.B. Mais expressed a very different opinion: 'Chesham is one of the ugliest towns it has ever been my misfortune to pass through. Why Cobbett liked it I don't know. It must have changed a great deal in 100 years'.

Despite being less than 30 miles from London, Chesham was isolated, off the main coach routes and without a railway until the end of the nineteenth century. The late arrival of the railway shaped the town; initial lack of transport facilities hindered industrial growth and many were self-employed in home-based crafts, based on local raw materials, mainly wood and leather, later in small workshops and factories among the homes of their workforce. Initial development was confined to the valley floor but when all the level ground was filled, house building started on the surrounding slopes, followed by the hilltops, a long climb from the town centre. The first chapter of this book illustrates Chesham's setting within the valley, with views from the hills and on the roads into the town.

Contrary to popular belief, Chesham does not mean 'the town on the river Chess', as the river, known in Saxon times as the *Isene* or, iron river, took its name from the town. Chesham was originally called *Caesteleshamm*, or the water meadow by the stone-heap, both of which are met in the second chapter, which portrays the old town. Known at Domesday as *Cestreham*, this gradually became corrupted to Chesham. The heart of old Chesham is the area near the parish church, built in the twelfth century on a mound which had probably seen Pagan worship centuries before that. Church Street, once the commercial centre of the town, and, adjacent to it, Germain Street, contain most of Chesham's oldest houses, which date from the fourteenth century onwards.

Chesham's main street starts from the foot of Amersham Road as Red Lion Street and leads through Market Square, continuing as High Street, much of which was built over the culverted river and includes the wide space of Broadway, all of which, until the coming of the railway, was mainly residential in character.

Broadway was the traditional site for special events, celebrations and the horse market. Attracted by the station bringing people in and out of the area, many shops and other businesses moved there from Church Street in the 1890s and most of the High Street properties were rebuilt or at least refronted for commercial purposes. The development of the High Street area is shown in Chapter Three, together with some of the events in Broadway.

At the lower end of Chesham the river turns through the wider valley of Waterside, with its own separate history dating back over a thousand years to when Lady Elgiva, the wife of King Edwy, first diverted the river to power the Lord's mill. Confusingly Waterside is the name of both the main road beside the river and the community through which it passes, pictured in Chapter Four.

Towards the end of Victoria's reign, with the expansion of industry brought about by the railway service, Chesham filled all the available area of level ground in the old town and began to spread up the valley, creating Newtown (pictured in Chapter Five) which, following Chesham's traditional pattern, consisted of a mixture of houses, workshops and mills. Due to the convenience of workplaces among the houses, commuting out of Chesham was still not considered, despite the convenience of the railway service and until well into the twentieth century there were those who thought a visit to Amersham was a great adventure. The final section contains pictures of ordinary Chesham folk, working or playing, mainly in unknown locations.

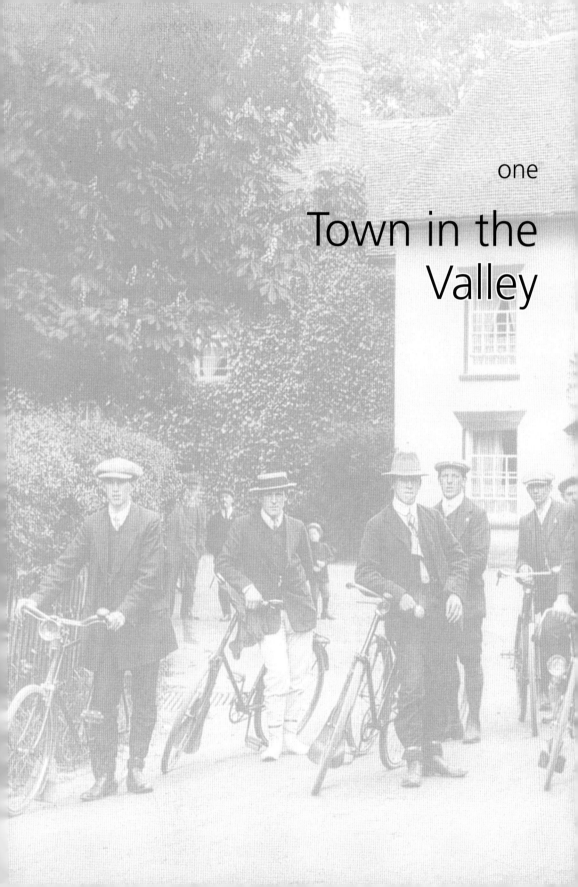

one

Town in the
Valley

The approach from Latimer along the valley of the River Chess is the only level road into Chesham, which here runs into Waterside along the north bank of the river. This 1905 postcard features the private bridge across the broad water of the stream below Weirhouse Mill, leading to the town's early sewage works.

The wide valley floor at the further part of Waterside is mostly occupied by the natural river and its man-made branches feeding many acres of artificial lakes where gravel had been extracted. This is also where, when pictured from the slopes of Chesham Bois in 1910, the best watercress was grown in the clear, iron-rich water.

The south-west facing slopes of Dungrove Hill were cultivated by medieval farmers whose repeated ploughing created The Balks, a series of parallel terraces along the hill-side. The highest of these is now partly occupied by Chesham's Cottage Hospital, to the right of this 1900s view, along the Waterside valley toward the town centre and church.

This view across the southern end of the High Street and the old town to the church on its ancient mound was photographed around 1935 from the slope of Dungrove Hill, above the platform of Chesham Station.

CHURCH AND PARK. CHESHAM.

From slightly further north in the same field, this view across the station building includes the whole width of the town with the church and the avenue of elm trees across the middle of the park, pictured in the late 1930s.

At the top of Dungrove Hill, some 200ft above the centre of the town, is historic Dungrove Farm the one-time home of Thomas Harding, the martyr of Chesham, who was burnt at the stake in 1532 for the heresy of reading the English translation of The Bible. A narrow belt of trees shelter the farm from the prevailing wind.

This 1930s panorama of Newtown clearly shows the workshops mixed in among the houses so that most of the craftsmen lived within walking distance of their workplaces. Earlier in the century the view included many more tall chimneys both of the steam engines which powered most of the older machinery and of the electricity-generating station which supplied power to the more up-to-date factories – but only a few then remained. The first houses of the new Pond Park Estate can be seen in the top right corner of the picture, with the cemetery field just below them.

Further north, the early seventeenth-century Nashleigh Farm is pictured around 100 years ago. The farm, near the top of Nashleigh Hill, which climbs steeply out of the Newtown valley as the main road to Berkhamsted, initially prospered by growing grain for the London market despite the difficulty of transport there.

In March 1926 the heaviest snowfall in the district for many years effectively isolated Chesham from the surrounding villages for several days and some minor roads were blocked for weeks. Chesham photographer Sydney Jowett struggled up Nashleigh Hill to photograph the drifts which reached well up the signpost at the top of the hill.

At the end of Newtown the road continues up Chesham Vale to the ridge hamlets to the north of Chesham. The former river valley is now normally dry except after excessive rainfall. This popular inn, the Black Horse, stands in the Vale about half a mile out of town.

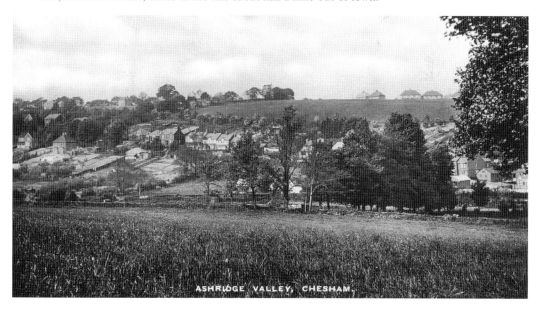

ASHRIDGE VALLEY, CHESHAM,

A branch of the main valley rises gently to the village of Ashridge. In 1927 the council bought a site in that valley for house building but when part of the adjoining hill came on the market, Pond Park Estate was started instead. Hivings Hill runs across this 1928 view over the valley, with the beginnings of Pond Park Road visible behind the dense trees.

Starting from the Broadway and initially bordering the park, Chartridge Lane climbs westward to that village. This 1912 view toward Chesham includes West's Barn beside the lane which ran through open countryside all the way until ribbon development started along it in the 1920s.

Further south the Missenden Road enters Chesham through Church Street. This 1905 photograph is of Halfway House, a farm nearly a mile along the valley out of Chesham where the road begins climbing into the hills but nowhere near halfway to anywhere!

From the hillside near Halfway House, this 1948 view along the Missenden Road into Chesham includes the Bury mansion in front of the sunlit church and the rest of the old town in the shade below Dungrove. To the right of the road, the ground was then being cleared for further council house-building.

In its remote valley Chesham was not on any of the turnpike roads and the main route into Chesham was the road from Amersham. Until the nineteenth century this was still only a rough track down the hillside through Beech Wood, the right-hand lane in this 1925 postcard view, which entered the town beside Amy Mill.

The main Amersham Road, built in 1820, was pictured here around 100 years later when it was still known as New Road. Waterside lies in the valley to the right of the view, with Dungrove Hill behind seen across an open field, which is now used for growing Christmas trees.

Near the foot of the hill is Chesham House, a Gothic-style building of 1880, pictured twenty-five years later. Until the 1934 boundary revision took place, it was outside Chesham, being just over the border in Chesham Bois. It was renamed Chesham Bois Manor in 1910 when the owner, then chairman of the local magistrates, purchased that village's manorial rights.

Amersham Road enters Chesham past Amy Mill House, pictured here aound 1900 when members of the Cestreham Cycle Club, one of the oldest in the country, were preparing to set off up the hill. The mill ceased working around 1860 but the mill house remained and was later extended. It was used as a hospital in the Second World War but was demolished in the 1970s. (CTMP)

On the way into Chesham, immediately after the mill, the Amersham Road crosses the River Chess by this bridge. Here a more modern cycle was pictured against the side of the bridge by a member of the Greenford Cycle Club while on a ride through the Chilterns in 1948. Over the brick parapet, the stream can be seen flowing past the watercress beds, which replaced the mill-pond.

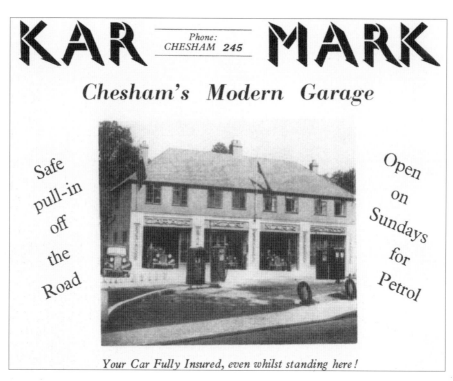

KAR — MARK

Phone: CHESHAM 245

Chesham's Modern Garage

Safe pull-in off the Road

Open on Sundays for Petrol

Your Car Fully Insured, even whilst standing here!

Over the river and into the town, this new garage was built beside the main road on part of the gardens of Mineral Cottage. Advertising here in a 1947 fête programme, it had recently been constructed by a local builder. A service station still occupies the site.

Just beyond the garage and set back behind mature trees is Mineral Cottage, pictured here around 1905. It is a relic of the 1820 plan to promote Chesham as a spa town, exploiting the curative properties of water from an adjacent spring. Ornamental gardens were laid out, including a watergarden fed by the nearby river but the scheme came to nothing.

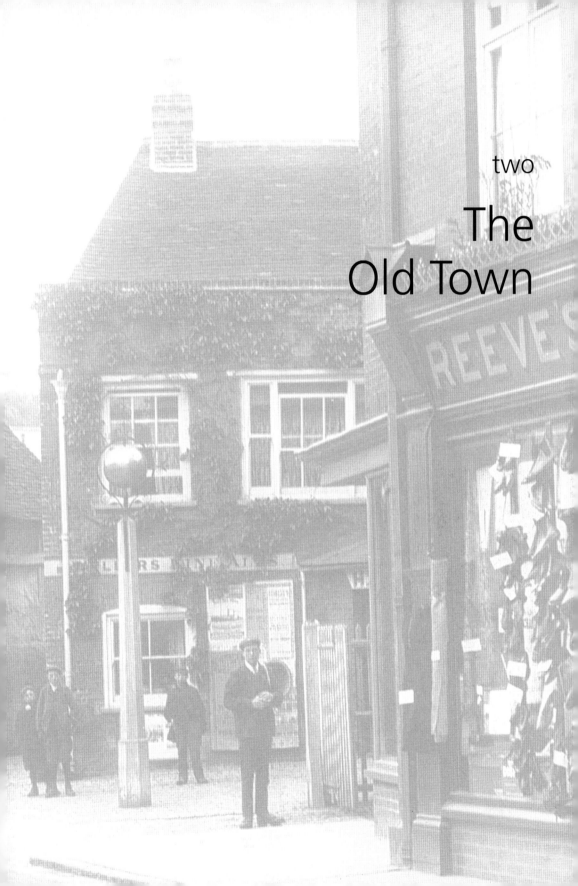

two

The
Old Town

Church Street starts from Market Square with Reeve's clothing shop and the Golden Ball Inn, pictured during the First World War. John Reeve used his outfitting shop to dispose of unclaimed objects from his pawnbrokers shop further down the street. The landlord of the inn was Harry Wing, a popular Chesham character who was also an 'authorised horse slaughterer' and unofficial vet.

Looking past the Golden Ball the next dozen or so cottages in Church Street were all built in the seventeenth century. When pictured in 1935, four of them were still small shops, a relic of the days before the railway when Church Street was the commercial centre of Chesham, with eight pubs, the post office and many shops.

Further up Church Street, pictured in 1940, Reynold's shop, where boots and shoes had been made since 1920, stood next to the entrance to Barnes motor body works, who were established in 1848 as coach builders. On the other side of the road, the narrow opening was Parsonage Lane where most of the cottages leading up to the park had been demolished under a 1935 slum clearance order.

The timber-framed Sun was built in the sixteenth century and initially provided lodgings for pilgrims visiting the nearby church. Pictured around 1900 it was then still licensed, but selling St Albans Beer rather than the local brew. Closed in 1937, it was then carefully dismantled and rebuilt as a country house a couple of miles away at Pednor.

Bury Lane, a short cul-de-sac off Church Street, leads to a terrace of former Lowndes' estate-workers' cottages known as the 'sixpenny houses' from their original weekly rent. Backing onto the park, they were given with it to Chesham Council when the lower park was presented to the town in 1953. Their backs are seen here from the park in about 1960.

Chesham Park was originally the private park of the Elizabethan Bury Hill House, standing above The Avenue near the church. This 1770 drawing greatly exaggerates the size of its lake created at the beginning of that century. The Lowndes family of The Bury acquired Bury Hill from the Skottowes in 1804 and immediately demolished the house.

The upper park contained Catling's Farm, also known as Park Farm, and their cattle had free access to the waters of the pond. As seen in this 1900 photograph, the pond was nothing like the artist's impression; it was really quite small with natural grassy edges sloping into the water, supplied by a nearby spring and overflowing into the Chess.

The Avenue was first planted in 1715 and had reached maturity, the trees forming 'an almost perfect Gothic arch', when many were uprooted by a hurricane in 1836. Replanted with young trees in 1845, the double line of Dutch Elms had reached a magnificent size when they were pictured here during winter around 1905. Threatened by the epidemic of Dutch Elm disease, they were felled in 1950.

In the harder winters of the early 1900s the lake regularly froze over and the Lowndes family allowed local residents to skate on the ice for a fee of twopence or a penny for children, and free on Sundays! Skating was a pastime that was very popular with the younger members of the town's population as this photograph demonstrates.

Bad winter conditions returned on 26 April 1908 when a freak storm brought several inches of snow over much of the county. In this view across the pond to the houses of Parsonage Lane and the outhouses of the High Street, a small boy has created an outsize snowball on the grass between the avenue and the pond.

During the First World War, members of the 126th Company of the Royal Engineers, while billeted in Chesham, practiced laying light railway lines over the marshy ground of The Moor, and bridge–building across the pond in the park. This card, sent in April 1915 by one of the men to his father, proudly notes that this is 'a view of the bridge we built last week'.

A group of soldiers from the 3/5 Suffolk Regiment who were then camped at Halton are pictured here on an outing to the Chesham bowling green on 26 August 1916. One of the men sent this card, commenting that it had turned very cold and asking the recipient to note his clean shirt.

THE LAKE, CHESHAM PARK

In 1920 the council leased the lower park from the Lowndes family and deepened the pond by removing tons of accumulated silt. They then provided two four-seater rowing boats which were hired out from a new landing stage at the Blucher Street end at a shilling an hour. In the 1930s the price was raised to half a crown but demand was such that a further two boats were added. The boats were kept secure overnight on the island from where the park keeper returned to dry land in a small dinghy.

Viewed from near the church gates, this was the scene in the late 1920s after Skottowes Pond, named after its original owners, had been given a concrete edge and surrounding path. The island was also enlarged and edged with elm boards to serve as a refuge for the resident ducks. The geese, which later took over the pond, were the descendants of tame birds misguidedly released there.

Also in the 1920s a circular terrace, where the town band later gave informal concerts on Sunday afternoons, was laid out between the avenue and the pond. The terrace was surrounded by a rose garden and connected to the pond by a flight of stone steps under a rustic pergola.

Further improvements to the area included swings and a sand-pit added in 1928 and a shelter alongside the avenue a few years later when children's facilities were also greatly increased. This photograph of the upper park was published in the late 1930s. The Lowndes family gave the whole park to the town to celebrate the 1953 coronation.

Published around 1850, this picture of St Mary's church, before its 1868 restoration, is a drawing of the view from Dungrove. It includes some of the town, shown as rooftops between the lower trees, but omits the houses nearer the church. The artist has, however, included part of the avenue of trees to the right of the little building in the churchyard.

The church's tower and south porch dominate this 1925 view from The Bury. The tower contains the original clock mechanism and a carillon which plays the hymn tune *St Sylvester* twice daily. Chesham was one of the last English towns to sound the curfew bell, which was rung at eight o'clock every weekday evening between Michaelmas and Easter until it was stopped at the outbreak of the Second World War.

Raised on its mound, the tower of St Mary's church is visible from all over the town. This 1900 telephoto view from the lower slopes of Dungrove Hill also includes the market hall's clock and lantern. Chesham's Saxon name, *Ceasteleshamme*, meant the water meadow by the stone heap, the latter being the church mound where the puddingstones buried in its foundations are believed to be the remains of a pagan place of worship.

GENERAL VIEW CHESHAM

This 1925 photograph from the tower looks back over the old town to Dungrove Hill. The rectory roof is at the bottom of the picture and High Street runs along below the belt of trees, with the town hall to the right of centre. Many of the old buildings were demolished to make way for St Mary's Way which today slices through the middle of this scene.

Pictured around 1920 the interior was then just as the 1868 restorers had left it, with the Victorian Gothic pulpit that replaced one of three tiers and the organ that was newly installed in the west gallery in 1852 moved to the north transept. The pews also date from that time when the high pews of 1606, in which parishioners dozed undisturbed, were ripped out.

This 1920s photograph shows two church wardens standing outside the fifteenth-century West Door of St Mary's church. The doors still bear the scars of bullets fired during the Civil War when Chesham was firmly on the Parliamentary side. No battles were fought there, so the bullet holes may be the result of high spirits or unofficial target practice by troops quartered in the town.

Above: The cobbled church path continues down past the Vicarage between the pillared gates and into Church Street, with the National School of 1845 on the right. The National School had become the Church Rooms before the end of that century. The Vicarage on the left was built on part of the churchyard in 1769 by the Duke of Bedford, who then held the patronage.

Right: Church Street curves round the foot of the church hill and contains most of Chesham's oldest houses. Almost next to the school, these three cottages with dormer windows were built of brick and timber around 1650 as a single house. Pictured in the 1900s, an un usual feature is the heavy shutters that hang down from hinges on the ground floor windows.

Left: Chesham's oldest house was divided into two, one half being Henry Burton's confectionery shop when it was pictured here in 1910. It was built in the fourteenth century of timber with wattle and daub infilling. Built originally as a hall house, it is described as an excellent example of domestic building of that period, a notable feature being the wooden tracery on the gabled wall.

Below: Chesham's big house, The Bury, stands in extensive grounds adjoining the churchyard. This 1905 picture shows the drive from Church Street, with two lodges inside the gates. The house was built in 1716 for William Lowndes, Secretary to the Treasury in the reign of Queen Anne. His successors, all great benefactors to the town, lived there until after the Second World War.

Posted in 1910, this card shows a meet of the Old Berkeley (West) Hunt setting off down the drive from The Bury where they had assembled on the front lawn. The hunt master was William Tyrwhitt-Drake of Shardeloes, a fellow magistrate, who held a similar position in Amersham to that of Squire William Frith-Lowndes in Chesham.

The gardens of The Bury were generously made available for local charities including, between the wars, the annual fête in aid of the Cottage Hospital, a highlight in Chesham's social calendar. This event included children's sports, various displays and side-shows in numerous tents and ended with dancing to the music of the town band, pictured here in 1928, and fireworks over the lake. (CTMP)

The Bury Pond, fed by a spring, one of the sources of the River Chess, extends for about 1/3 mile from the mansion and roughly in the middle is a small island, that can be reached by a foot-bridge. On the island were two boathouses, one of which is pictured here in its beautiful wooded setting around 1905.

Posted as a Christmas greeting card in 1914, the town band is seen here playing in a clearing on the island with The Bury mansion in the distance. They have chosen an idyllic, but remote place to play as if, perhaps, they didn't want an audience, but they attracted a small group of listeners on the waterside path.

A part of Pednor Road, which skirts the grounds of The Bury close to Bury Pond, is known as Frogmore. Frogmore was a popular viewpoint for taking pictures of the mansion, with the church tower behind it. In this Glimpse of The Bury photographed in the 1930s, the pond is hidden from view by the roadside bank.

Across Pednor Road this willow-lined stream is another source of the Chess. Fed from a spring near Halfway House Farm it flows placidly through the fields where it joins the Bury Pond's overflow. Below the gentle waterfall, pictured around 1950, the water passes under Missenden Road, alongside Water Lane, and joins the main stream from Higham Mead near Town Bridge.

In May 1918, a torrential rainstorm over Pednor turned the normally dry Pednor Bottom into a raging torrent, the deep water sweeping away everything in its path and flooding Pednormead End to a depth of 3ft. This photograph shows the aftermath of the flood with the fallen trees then sawn into manageable lengths and sections of brickwork still littering the road.

Such floods were not uncommon in the low-lying parts of the town, as heavy rainfall in the surrounding hills flowed down one of the several valleys, which centre on Chesham, turning the main streets into rivers. This pair of photographs shows the flood damage to an old cottage in the same area in 1917.

This 1905 view from Church Street into the start of Missenden Road includes the original Lowndes' estate–workers' cottages on the right. Only the furthest of these, an 1842 modernisation of a timber-framed cottage, was retained when the rest of the terrace was replaced in 1919 by mock–Tudor houses round a small courtyard.

Germain Street leads from another corner of Market Square into the old town but is not so obviously old as Church Street. Pictured in 1928, the Red Lion Inn was then a square building at the end of Germain Street next to a block of shops. The shops, as far as the parked car, were demolished in 1937 and a new Red Lion was built behind the old, which was then removed to ease the bottleneck at Red Lion Corner.

The three-storey building on the right in the previous picture was then and still remains the home of *The Bucks Examiner*, Chesham's first local newspaper. Facing its offices this large house, which is clearly in less than perfect condition but had extensive grounds, was up for sale when it was photographed in 1936. It was replaced by the Embassy Cinema, which opened the following year.

The 1930s frontage of the Embassy Cinema extended over the flanking shops, and the interior, which was much admired for its decor and style, included an elegant café. Despite the earlier closure of its only rival, audiences dwindled in the 1970s and the cinema closed in 1982. This photograph was taken shortly after its closure.

Germain Street crosses the River Chess by Town Bridge, pictured in the 1950s. Over the bridge is the garden wall of The Meades where, in the eighteenth century, the Mead family's tannery used a watermill to grind tannin from tree bark. Beyond there is the entrance to King Street, with more of Chesham's oldest houses, which just escaped a clearance order before the First World War.

Duck Alley was a terrace of cottages alongside the river downstream from Town Bridge. There had been a proposal to rename it Riverside Terrace but the traditional name was retained until the dwellings were demolished under a clearance order in the 1930s. This picture was taken from the bridge during the demolition with only the far end of the terrace still standing.

Looking back towards town from Water Lane, this is the more familiar view of Town Bridge, a scene which has been drawn, painted and photographed countless times and has appeared on dozens of postcards like this one, which was printed around 1920. The gentle slope into the stream, which was then covered with shallow water, is now usually covered with parked cars, there being less water in the river now.

Water Lane is no more than a footpath beside this length of river known as The Bury Brook, which leads to the saw-mill. Loads of newly delivered tree trunks, hauled along the stream bed from Town Bridge by horses and later by traction engines, were piled up in front of the mill.

Looking from Water Lane around 1900, level snow covers the Water Meadow with the church behind it on its heap of stones, the two elements of Chesham's original name. The risk of frequent flooding inhibited building on this low-lying land until the creation of Water Meadow car park there in the 1960s, which ruined the most attractive scene near the town centre.

Above and opposite below: On the site of a bark mill and tannery, William Wright's sawmill was established in 1842 and General Saw Mills in Water Lane was one of three Chesham firms advertising in 1877 as manufacturers of Cricket Bats, Trundle Hoops, Toy Spades, Sieve Hoops, Brush Boards, Spoons, Handled and Round Bowls and Butter Prints, and so on. Pictured here around 1920, this mill continued in operation until it was demolished in 1965. The opposite picture shows the raw material on the area at the edge of the stream, from where an overhead gantry transferred it to the power saws, and in the photograph above two craftsmen are putting the finishing touches to wooden wheels. (CTMP)

The New Footpath, which was not very new when this picture was published in 1910, is an early Victorian lane leading off Germain Street. It is, however, much newer than some of the cottages there which date from as far back as the late sixteenth century; the nearest house on the Germain Street Corner was Chesham's first workhouse.

Above: The Church of England Infants' School was built in 1851 on the site of the tithe barn beside the New Footpath. It had the capacity for 115 pupils. Under the 1902 Education Act it was taken over by the county council and in 1911 was rebuilt to take 200 infants and 250 boys. Pictured aroumd 1915, it also housed a practical training centre for woodwork, cookery and housecraft.

Above and opposite below: These early 1900s photographs of the infants were taken in the original building of Germain Street School where they appear to be enjoying themselves. Many Chesham people have less happy memories of the rebuilt school as it included the surgery of the dreaded school dentist.

Beyond the school where the road begins to climb gently out of town, this part of Germain Street had been renamed Fullers Hill after the family who owned Germains for 200 years. Photographed in 1900, this line of old cottages extends back to Germains' house. The land around Germains' extended behind the cottages to Wey Lane and included the site of a first-century Roman village.

Germains, Chesham

Pictured around 1910 the house Germains, or Great Germains as it had been known, which stands alongside Fullers Hill, is a mainly eighteenth-century house with a medieval timber-framed wing. Some 200 yards further on past a group of modern houses, Little Germains, of similar age, is the last house before the road enters open country on its way over the hills to Hyde Heath.

On Fullers Hill. Chesham

A gate in the road side hedge almost opposite Germains gives access to a footpath across a large open field and on to Beech Wood and the old road to Amersham. This 1930s photograph shows horse power is being used to gather the last of the crop from this field, against a background of the trees in the valley.

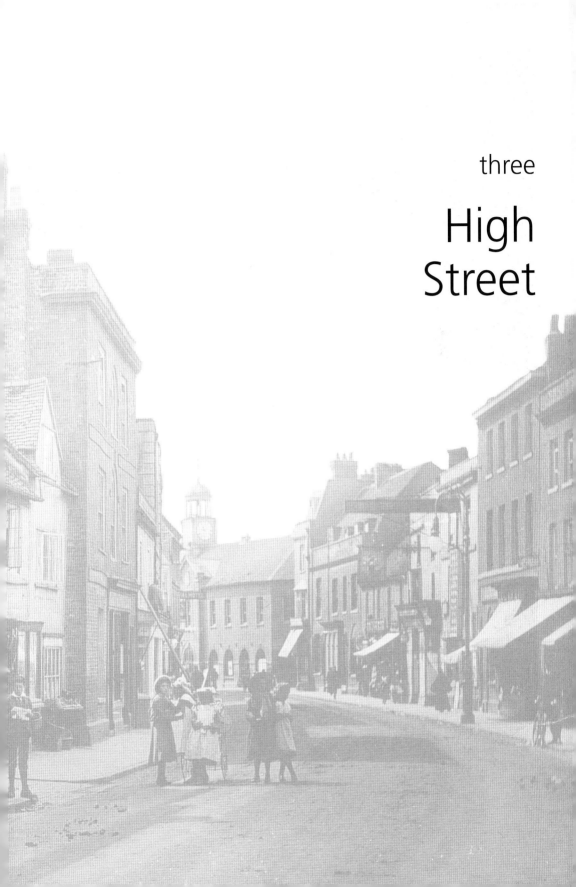

three

High Street

The High Street continues to the south as Red Lion Street, as far as the site of the ancient pound at the junction of Waterside and the Amersham Road. This view of the junction from the garden beside Amersham Road dates from 1939 just after the widening of the main road from here to Market Square.

Looking the other way around the same date, Waterside branches off left as Amersham Road sweeps round the ornamental garden created on the surplus of the land acquired for the road-widening scheme. Behind the garden, watercress beds occupied the lake which once reached from The Meades to Amy Mill and which, in 1979, became The Meades Water Gardens.

Pictured in 1918, the Chesham Scout Troop, led by their band, is marching along Red Lion Street on the way to a service at Christ Church in Waterside, apparently followed by a horse-drawn caravan. As the only scout band in the London area, they were invited to take part in the Lord Mayor's Show. To the left of the caravan is the Nag's Head, one of the buildings later lost to road widening.

In 1930 these Red Lion Street shops stood between the Nag's Head on the left and the Red Lion out of view to the right. Warner's shop not only sold a wide range of sweets but made many of the most popular ones on the premises. Beyond the Nag's Head, the pub's yard, which faced two Baptist chapels across the road, had been the venue for sheep markets in the 1890s.

Opposite the Red Lion, Townfield Yard led off Red Lion Street up toward the railway and along behind the east side of that street. At the top of the slope, this pair of houses, derelict when photographed in 1931, stood beside the entrance to Jacob's Ladder, steps up to The Balks and Dungrove via a footbridge over the railway line.

Around the corner of Townfield Yard these run-down terraces faced each other across an untidy yard with a central drain gulley. Photographed shortly after the whole yard had been made the subject of a clearance order, nearly all the terraces were demolished in 1935 and replaced by a model village of residences for old people, which was simply called Townfield.

Next to Townfield was Stratford's Yard, named after Edmund Stratford who made woodware there around 1850. When it was photographed in 1905 a later Stratford ran a building firm. His creeper-clad cottage was a timber-framed sixteenth-century building. It escaped the 1932 clearance order but slowly decayed over the next twenty years after which it was demolished.

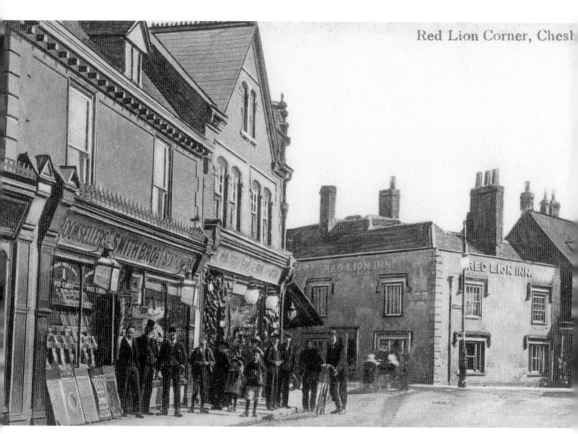

Red Lion Corner, Chest

Until the 1937 road-widening scheme, a traffic bottleneck was created in the centre of this view where Red Lion Street enters Market Square. During the road-widening the old Red Lion was demolished and its replacement set back from the widened road. This postcard was published around 1910 by Smith Brothers who gathered a large group of customers outside their stationery shop for the photograph. Next door to Smith's, the Oak Tree Boot & Shoe shop was the retail branch of Reynolds', the Blucher Street boot manufacturers.

In another 1910 postcard by Smith Brothers, Market Square is seen here from the Red Lion. The square was laid out in the thirteenth century when the market charter was granted. The market hall, which dates from the eighteenth and nineteenth century and contained a meeting room above an open market piazza, was demolished in 1965 as part of a traffic improvement scheme, a proposal first raised in 1939.

The other side of Market Square is seen here in 1938 when two butchers occupied adjacent shops at the left edge. In the era of the town's horse-drawn fire engine, part of the piazza was used as the fire station and, in the 1930s with the arches blocked, it became a 'walk-around store' and later a textile factory. The meeting room had also served as the town hall and an early cinema.

The main building in this postcard view into the High Street from Market Square is the Crown Hotel, built of light and dark local bricks in a chequered pattern. Known to have been functioning in the sixteenth century, the Crown served as local headquarters for the Parliamentary forces during the Civil War. When pictured around 1930, it advertised itself as a 'family and commercial hotel' serving 'hot and cold luncheons and teas' with accommodation for parties of sixty and was recognised by the AA, RAC, CTC and RAOB. The carriage arch, then surrounded by road signs, gave access to the former stables used as garages for visitors' cars. The Crown was demolished around 1960 and replaced by a small supermarket.

Above: Next door to the Crown was H. Thomas' millinery and drapery shop. This photograph was taken in 1911 when he had only recently taken over from the Aitken family who had run it for fifty years. As well as dresses, blouses and accessories, the window displayed many handmade notices, announcing 'Always The Latest Hats', 'Styles of Distinction & Good Taste' and 'The Smartest of New Fashions', and so on.

Right: Next door at No.5 and also pictured around 1911, Frederick Bendall ran a tobacconist shop as a sideline to his main business as a hairdresser. One window was full of hair lotions, around a dummy sporting the latest ladies hair style, while the other displayed countless varieties of tobacco and cigarettes. The faded notice between the upstairs windows advertises: Ladies Hairdressing and Singeing Sixpence.

Both sides of the High Street are seen on this 1920 postcard including, on the left, two of the town's popular family-run shops. First is Wallace's ironmongery which, for fifty years, stocked a vast range of household requirements and also provided a plumbing service. Piggin's grocery, next door, also remained a family business for well over forty years.

This 1950 view of the next section of High Street includes, partly hidden behind the delivery dray, the George and Dragon Inn that was always known simply as the George. The inn dates from the seventeenth century and was the terminus of the accommodation coach to London until 1845, when it became so for The Chesham & Rickmansworth Railway Coach, which connected at Watford with London trains.

Opposite the George was Pattersons' drapery who issued this advertising postcard in 1909. David Graham Patterson started the business in 1873 in Townsend Road, soon opening a second shop in Church Street. They moved to the High Street in 1901, and, continued by subsequent generations of the family, the business expanded into the adjoining premises remaining there until the 1960s.

Looking further into High Street in 1950 from under the ancient wrought-iron brackets holding the George's hanging sign, the National Provincial Bank is considered one of the better modern buildings in the street. It was built in 1912 for their predecessors, the Union of London and Smith's Bank, on the site of Butcher's Bank, which they had taken over.

Looking back over the southern end of High Street, this 1920s view includes the distant market hall where the road bends into Market Square.

This 1950s postcards view of the next section towards Broadway includes, to the left of the parked car, Darvell's bakery. This family-run business started in 1838 in Church Street, opening a second shop in High Street when that became Chesham's main shopping centre. In 1912 they moved to the premises they still occupy today, with the bakery behind the shop.

A few doors further on, in the late 1920s, Vennall's jewellers and watchmakers advertised the 'famous Cestreham watches' around their shop-front clock. Next door W.E. Garlick's Central Pharmacy and opticians also stocked photographic and wireless outfits. Next door again was the Stag, which sold Aylesbury Brewery Co.'s ales and beers.

Back on the other side of the street, this three-storey house was occupied by the Chesham Conservative & Unionist Club from 1910 until they moved to Station Road in the 1930s when the house, in the centre of High Street, was rebuilt as a Woolworths store. Before the Conservatives, the building had housed a ladies' boarding school from the late 1880s.

This 1930s image shows the Stag which doubled as a greengrocers' shop, both reached through the same front door enabling secret drinkers to pretend they were only going in for a few vegetables. The Stag closed at the end of that decade and was converted into two shops. The next-door seventeenth-century shop with the gabled roof was then Charles How's china shop.

Staying with the old shop but going back in time it then belonged to another greengrocer, Arthur Hobbs, who was also a confectioner. This card was sent by the shop owners to their daughter whilst they were on holiday in 1911; the card asks her to guess who was standing in the doorway. Later that year they moved the greengrocery to other premises nearer the market hall.

This view back into High Street dates from the 1940s. John Tree had kept the drapery at No.50 from around 1900 when the tall house next door belonged to Dr John Chuchill, a popular GP and surgeon to the Cottage hospital. The doctor's house, known as the tree house from one in the small front garden, became The House of Tree when the drapery expanded into it in 1920.

When the railway was built into Chesham in the late 1880s, Station Road was carved through the side of High Street to give access to the new station on the hillside up behind the shops. This picture of the station and the signal box was taken in the late 1950s, the last days of steam on the line, but it had hardly altered externally from the day it opened in 1889.

This 1905 view of the station platform from the hillside includes the posed station staff, six men and a dog. The base of the water tower is covered with posters with dozens more on every available space on the walls under the awning. At the far end of the platform, a pile of parcels awaits despatch in the guards' van of the next suitable train.

Pictured in the late 1930s, the crew pose beside the engine of the 'shuttle' train, ready to return to Chalfont and Latimer. In the background, the signal box is seen over the poster boards. As well as controlling the run-around movements to return the engine to the front of reversing trains, the signalman looked after traffic in and out of the busy goods yard beyond the station.

This view from the footbridge near Jacob's Ladder was taken in 1961 after electrification but before delivery of the new silver trains. Here the shuttle is standing at the second platform, which was added the previous year as a short-lived experiment to allow the three-car shuttle and a London train to stand in the station together. The extra track was laid over part of the station's prize garden.

In this 1920 view over Station Road and Broadway, the white building is the Empire Cinema next to the goods yard. Films had been shown at the Market Hall, but this, the town's first real cinema, opened in 1912. Later faced with competition from the better-equipped Chesham Palace in Broadway, it closed in 1920, was then used for light industry and was later demolished.

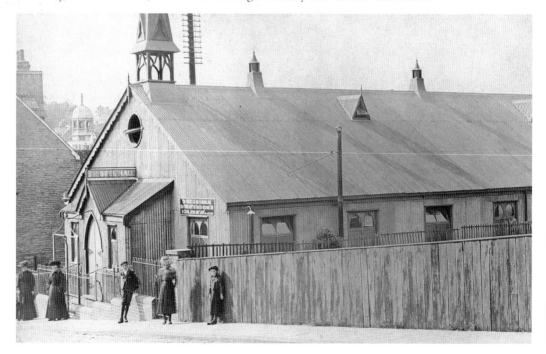

Next door down Station Road, the corrugated iron Gospel Hall had been built in 1890. When pictured in the 1920s the ornamental spire was dwarfed by a telegraph pole serving the east side of Broadway. Later rebuilt in more durable materials, the Gospel Hall still fulfils its original purpose.

This 1927 aerial photograph shows the layout of Broadway with High Street entering from the right (south) and continuing as Upper High Street to the left, all following a single house numbering sequence. The following pictures show Broadway buildings in clockwise sequence starting from High Street and with a detour west into Blucher Street at the lower edge of the view. These are followed by a selection of pictures showing special events in Broadway, which has been the traditional setting for fairs, the Guy Fawkes bonfire, pronouncements and celebrations from the days when, as Pillory Green, Broadway saw the public punishment of petty criminals.

Starting from Tree's shop, these were the next buildings on the west side of Broadway. In the centre of this 1899 view the recently-built Lamb Inn, which initially displayed its name on the roof-top, sold local beer and offered 'good stabling'. The post office occupied the shop beyond the Lamb for a few years and then moved across Broadway to Upper High Street.

In the 1930s, Mrs Atkins' Broadway Tea Rooms became an unofficial 'staff canteen' for the crews of the many buses which stood in Broadway between journeys. The London Transport bus at the stop was on route 397 to Tring shortly after London Transport had absorbed the Amersham bus company. Carlton Press, to the left edge in this photograph , had moved from the other side of The Lamb in the 1900s.

In around 1880, this was the view into Blucher Street where the sign of the One Star Inn is visible in front of the seventeenth-century cottages, which survived until the road works of the 1960s. Blucher Street was originally Bury Hill End, then Bridge Street, as it crossed a feeder stream of the River Chess, which then flowed into Broadway in front of the dark buildings. (CTMP)

By the time this building was photographed in 1895, the whole corner of Blucher Street had been rebuilt in uniform style with a rounded frontage on the actual corner, all of which still stands today. The shop next door to the Lamb was the retail outlet of Webb's brush works, established in 1829. The manufactory unit of Webb's brush works was based in Sills Yard behind their shop and was reached via the arch round the corner to the right.

Above and below: These two pictures show Robert Webb's brush manufactory behind their Broadway shop. The upper picture is a view of the works from the cobbled Sill's Yard. The lower picture is the interior of the shaping and drilling shop. All brush backs and handles were, of course, made from wood and it is said that brush-making in Chesham started as a way of using up the off-cuts from the town's other woodware industries. These photographs date from 1895 shortly before the works moved to new premises in Townsend Road, on the edge of Newtown, where they remained until 1982. At the time of their relocation, they were one of half-a-dozen brush factories in Chesham.

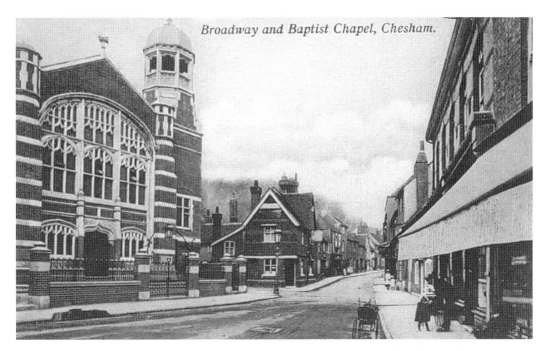

Broadway and Baptist Chapel, Chesham.

Looking into Blucher Street in 1910, the smart new Broadway Baptist church is a 1902 replacement for the original General Baptist Chapel of 1712. Between the church and the One Star Inn was the entrance to Star Yard, a cluster of fourteen small dwellings behind Blucher Street, which was demolished as 'slum clearance' and was the site of the town's first car park in 1938.

Published in the 1930s, this postcard view looking into town from the park gates includes the whole of Blucher Street. The old cottages on the right side of this short road included a pub at each end with the Blue Ball near the park and the One Star almost in Broadway with Star Yard behind them. Those on the left backed onto Reynolds' boot factory.

Left: This early 1930s photograph includes, on the left, No.1 Blucher Street, the only building now remaining in the street after the wholesale demolition to create St Mary's Way. It was, from 1899 until the 1950s, the Climpson family's wine shop. The next block, in Broadway, was then the headquarters of the Chesham & Wycombe Co-operative Society.

Below: In front of the cottages at the northern end of Broadway, this horse-trough, a gift from the Metropolitan Drinking Fountain & Cattle Trough Association, was installed in 1909 beside the old town pump. It not only refreshed horses, including some from nearby stables whose owners were too mean to lay on a water supply, but also topped up the tanks of passing traction engines.

BRANDON & SONS

. County . Furnishers

25,000 feet of Showrooms

Everything for
FURNISHING.
REMOVALS.
STORAGE.

Tel. 67 CHESHAM

FREE DELIVERY.

"The Stores where you
Spend to Save."

CHESHAM

The cottages in the previous scene were replaced in 1927 by Brandon's new building, the three matching bays in the main picture in this 1931 advertisement. The simpler left-hand part had been built beyond the cottages soon after the railway. The smaller pictures show their other premises, both on the east side of Broadway.

In this view of the north side of Broadway in 1930, the war memorial in front of Brandon's store serves as a bus stop for the Amersham & District service to Windsor. Next door is the Cock, just one of Chesham's seventy beer-houses for a population of 7,000 late in the nineteenth century. Beyond that, a pair of cottages is partly hidden by the National Bus Co.'s bus to Watford.

Until replaced by Barclays Bank in 1933, the cottages next to the Cock pub housed this pair of shops: Albert Henry Philbey, a tailor and breeches maker, started business in Upper High Street around 1890 and moved here a few years later. His neighbour, Alfred Peck, also moved here before the turn of the century from his previous bakery in Red Lion Street.

The east side of Broadway is seen here before Station Road was cut through, just past the horse and cart in this 1885 photograph. At this date all the buildings were private houses, although some of the occupiers sold a few goods from their front parlours. The only building still recognisable today is the small bay-windowed cottage with the low roof and dormer window. (CTMP)

By 1911, nearly every building had been refronted or rebuilt and, bar the shop fronts, the scene is similar to today's. Four houses had been replaced by Station Road and its flanking buildings, the tall square block on the left and the ornate bank building on the further corner. Behind the lamppost, E.G. Elliman was the first owner of the shop which has remained a chemist's ever since. Next door ironmonger George Potter Harding displays much of his stock on the pavement outside.

To the left in the previous picture, the decorated front of Cameo House, a building of the railway era, is the only one to display its 1890 construction date. To its left in this 1948 photograph, the Westminster Bank, with integral manager's house, had been built in the late 1920s on the site of an auctioneer's shop and Wallis's shoeing forge.

Left: Cameo House was occupied by Mayo's tobacconists shop and next door, in the original small cottage, was another tobacconists, started by Edmund Sanders in 1895 and continued by Laceys from 1935 onwards. This second tobacconists served many passengers waiting for buses at the stop immediately outside, where, in this 1950 picture, a Bedford Duple coach of the local Rover Bus Co. has just arrived from Hemel Hempstead.

Below: This view from Brandon's Store dates from 1935 when the area outside the store was used as a car park. Behind the war memorial was the Astoria cinema and, beyond it, the gabled shop-front led to Paramount Stores' showroom on the hillside behind. On the other side of the road, Chesham Electric Light & Power Co. sold apparatus in the corner shop with the curved frontage. (CTMP)

Left: With an Amersham & District bus parked by the war memorial, the Chesham Palace cinema is pictured here in 1930, shortly before it was renamed the Astoria. It had been opened in 1914 by Chesham Picture Palace and Concert Hall Ltd with a full stage and dressing rooms in addition to the film screen. Two small shops, then used by Brandons, were incorporated in the street frontage.

Below: The Original Chesham Coffee Tavern occupied the twin-gabled building near Station Road for twenty years from 1890. Pictured here in 1900, owner William Ivory stands in the doorway beside notices of their opening times – they were open until 11 p.m. on weekdays – and their speciality, Prime Ham and Cold Joints always in cut. (CTMP)

John Thomas' tailor shop in the old building on the corner of Station Road was completely destroyed in May 1891 by a fire which also damaged the recently opened coffee tavern next door. The fire was only prevented from spreading further by the concerted effort of the volunteer fire brigade with the cooperation of the water company's engineer who turned up the pressure to the hydrants. This photograph shows the aftermath of the fire when only the Station Road wall remained standing. The site behind the shop was already for sale and the whole block was rebuilt with a suite of rooms in Station Road over the shop in Broadway.

The rebuilt Station Road corner was first occupied by the Chess Vale Temperance Hotel with Catling's shop underneath, pictured in 1905. Smith & Co., drapers, milliners, costumiers, silk mercers and furriers, took over the shop in 1910, who were in turn shortly replaced by International Stores, which remained there for forty years with the Chesham Club and Literary Institute above them until the mid-1930s.

Regular cattle and horse sales were held in Broadway before the First World War and at the opening of hostilities horses were collected there for war service. The newly built Chesham Palace is prominent in this view of the sale.

Following the armistice and the return of the surviving soldiers, a Peace Thanksgiving service was held in Broadway in 1919. The open-air service on 6 July was conducted from the steps of the Congregational church where the ministers from all of Chesham's many churches and chapels gathered.

As part of Chesham's Peace Celebration in 1919, a temporary war memorial cross was dedicated in Market Square. Then in 1921 the permanent memorial, paid for by public subscription, was unveiled in Broadway. It consists of the statue of a soldier standing easy on a plinth with bas-relief scenes representing the Navy and Air Force and the names of those from Chesham who lost their lives.

Here in 1922 a party of Chesham men and women, possibly on a works outing, is ready to set off in the Dennis charabanc *Albatross* from opposite the cinema.

In 1922, massed crowds in Broadway completely swamped a carnival procession trying to make its way south into High Street. Most of the participants are hidden by the crowd but Britannia can be seen with her trident to the left of the cinema.

A decade later and a smaller crowd stands well back from the carnival route as a decorated motor vehicle in the procession drives past, followed by a horse-drawn cart. The motor vehicle is so well covered with flags and flowers that the driver must have had great difficulty seeing the way.

Seen from Blucher Street, Broadway is well decorated for Chesham's celebration of the Royal Jubilee in 1935. Many of the decorations had probably been made in the town for George Tutill, one of the country's leading flag and banner makers who had been based in Higham Road since the mid-1920s.

Leaving Broadway and looking into Upper High Street in 1920, the first building on the right is a house built in 1625, which became Chesham's main post office in 1903. The further part was a butcher's in the nineteenth century. Beyond that was a mix of houses and businesses including an umbrella maker, a timber merchant, and, later, the Co-op departmental store.

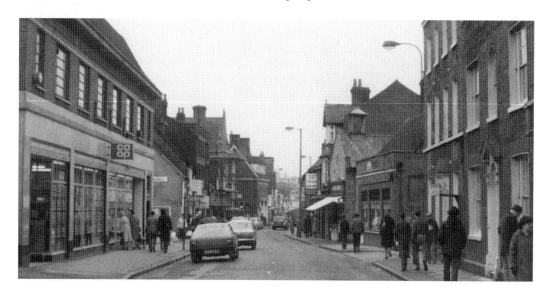

Chesham Equitable Co-operative Society was founded in 1875 with its first small shop in Germain Street. By 1900 it occupied large premises in Broadway and half-a-dozen small shops around the town. In the 1920s it took over Wycombe Co-op and later Tring to become Chilterns Co-op. Pictured in 1981, this smart modern store, opened in 1935, brought all departments under one roof.

The Nash Brothers' Chesham Brewery started life around 1840 at the end of Upper High Street on the corner of White Hill, also known as Hempstead Road, using water from a deep well on the site. Later amalgamated with Brackley Brewery, they were taken over by Ind Coope and closed in 1957. The buildings, pictured in their 1930 advert, were demolished in the 1960s.

The railway was built into Chesham for goods traffic as much as for passengers and a large goods yard was cut into the side of the hill with road access from White Hill. In this 1888 photograph, men are working on the roof of the goods shed there. Most of the incoming traffic was coal for the town's gas and electricity works and factories with local manufactures going out.

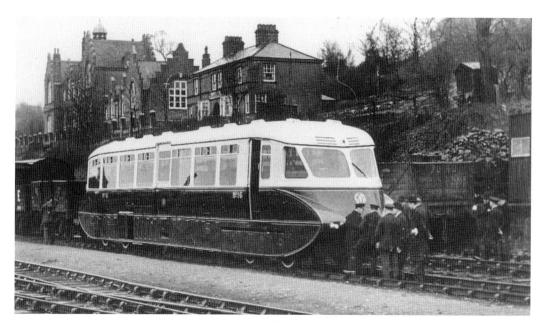

This 1936 view of the goods yard includes White Hill School to the left above the excavation. In the yard, a group of officials, some bowler-hatted, others in railway uniform, examine a diesel railcar which the local railway operators had borrowed from Great Western as an unsuccessful experiment to find a cheaper alternative to the steam-hauled shuttle.

In 1961 the Plough Inn stood on the corner of White Hill and Broad Street. Now only a memory, its name was perpetuated in The Plough filling station which replaced it. Beyond the Plough, the empty site and the next house were then being redeveloped as a parade of shops.

four

Waterside

Left: Looking back toward the Pound in the 1920s, Waterside is dominated by Hayes' boot factory. As early as 1850 there were five boot manufacturers in Chesham and James Hayes started soon afterwards, followed by John who built this factory in 1890. His sons continued the business until its closure, in the 1930s, due to a slump in the demand for their speciality heavy boots.

Below: On the south side of Waterside, and until 1934 officially in Chesham Bois, the Canada Works in Bois Moor Road was originally known as Bois Mill. From 1910 to 1925 the sawmill specialised in the production of portable poultry houses, later changing to the manufacture of tent pegs and mallets. Their yard was a wonderful playground for local children in 1920.

Left: In Waterside the river divides, the original stream beside Bois Moor Road along the southern side of the valley with the diverted mill-stream on the other. The shallow stream between Bois Moor Road and the island offered the chance to fish for tiddlers and take the occasional dip in the clear water. This postcard of a family group beside the water was posted in 1910.

Below: Back on the other side of the valley, one Metropolitan Railway goods cart is entering the yard of the Chiltern Toy Works with bales of fabric while another, loaded with their products, stands in Waterside with a third horse to help pull the heavy load up the steep hill to the goods yard. Pictured in 1923, many of the workers are standing on the factory steps. (CTMP)

Established in Newtown in 1908, H.G. Stone's Chiltern Toy Works occupied the Waterside premises from 1920 until the factory was diverted to war work twenty years later. Their main product was a wide range of teddy bears in various sizes and qualities and inside the works, local girls are busy stuffing the bodies, surrounded by crates of heads, arms and legs. (CTMP)

Photographed from the railway embankment in the early 1900s, a terrace of cottages runs uphill from Waterside to the foot of The Balks with the Cottage Hospital higher up. In a typical Chesham situation, the cottages overlook the woodyard of another small woodware factory. Chesham Gas Works, which first supplied the town in 1847, is just out of view to the right.

Chesham Cottage Hospital was built in 1869 and is shown here in 1915 before its enlargement as a War Memorial. It is on one of the upper levels of The Balks, nearly 100ft above the valley floor. Before the NHS, it was financed by 'penny a week' collections from most of the town's workforce, payments from wealthier patients and the annual fête at The Bury.

Above and right: Further along, another lane leads up the slope between the houses of Waterside. At the top of the line of small workshops, Inkerman Terrace runs along the hillside where the dwellings enjoyed a southerly aspect and a view across The Moor. One of the houses was the home of Fred Leach whose adjacent sawmill produced mainly spades and shovels and a range of wooden spoons. In the lower picture, the tree trunks appear to have been delivered almost to the front door of his house next to a flight of steps leading further up the hill side. (CTMP)

The River, Chesham,

W.H.A.1325.

This 1910 view from Waterside shows part of the two-acre mill-pond of Lord's Mill. Beyond it, The Moor, a marshy island between the artificially raised mill stream and the original river (at the foot of the railway embankment), was used for grazing both horses and the Aylesbury ducks whose off-spring were bred in the adjacent cottages.

A few years later, the Urban District Council replaced the rotting timbered edge of the pond with concrete which had a proper path on top. By popular request, they also planted a line of ornamental trees there in the 1920s to beautify the scene. In this early 1930s view, the trees are becoming well established.

Chesham Ducks.

Pictured on the bank of the mill-pond in the 1900s, a couple-of-dozen white Aylesbury ducks enjoy the freedom to swim in the clear Chess water. These were the breeding birds whose off-spring were denied that freedom, born and bred in the duck-breeder's shed or in his cottage and fattened on a special diet until table-ready at the age of eight weeks.

Waterside, Chesham.

Seen across the still water in the late 1920s, the huddle of shacks at the water's edge had, in Victoria's reign, been the centre of Chesham's duck-breeding industry. At its peak batches of plucked birds left daily for the London markets but the trade had virtually died out by this date. The shacks and neighbouring cottages were all replaced by Riverside Court in 1964.

Christ Church in Waterside was initially a mission church of St Mary's and was built out of flint and located in a prominent position overlooking the water above Lord's Mill in 1863. In 1867 Waterside became a parish in its own right and two years later a vicarage was built behind the church in Trapps Lane, its chimneys just visible to the right of the church roof.

Opposite the church, 'Kitty's Bridge' was erected across the mill stream near Lord's Mill. It gave pedestrians a short cut to the moor without using the narrow, and sometimes busy, road in front of the mill. Pictured around 1927 when the bridge was about five years old, the well-protected trees here had only recently been planted.

Above: A mammoth feat of engineering for its day, the mill pond was created over 1,000 years ago for the original Lord's Mill. The seventeenth-century mill building on the site with its massive undershot wheel, necessitated by the shallow head of water unusually placed across the stream, is pictured in 1900. Steam replaced water power soon afterwards and the mill worked until 1955.

The barn on the other side of the mill house has, since late in the nineteenth century, been used by engineering firms. From 1890, Cremer & Cheeld, mechanical and electrical engineers, millwrights and general mill furnishers, also provided 'electric bells, telephones, electric lighting, flour mill and saw mill machinery'. Pictured in 1895 with a selection of wheels outside in Bois Moor Road, Cheeld & Co. specialised in boring artesian wells, and a few years later they added motor car building to their range of activities. They also sold parts for an early kit-car, the 'English Mechanic' up-to-date petrol car at very reasonable prices, e.g. aluminium crank chamber at £2 15s and best steel crank shaft for £1.

Opposite below: The front of the mill is shown on this 1945 postcard view along the mill leat. In the 1960s it was threatened by a proposal to divert Waterside traffic across the Moor but the plan was abandoned and the mill remained and slowly decayed after it ceased working, until it was demolished in the 1980s. The adjoining miller's house, of similar age, was maintained and still stands.

In 1895 the road outside the mill house was obstructed by a thatch-roofed outhouse. To its right in this picture was a group of old cottages, the furthest of which were terraced alongside the mill leat. All were replaced in 1933 by a single terrace facing the mill. Beyond these, the lower slope beside the road was cultivated with open fields above.

Looking downstream from the mill in 1900, the children are sitting on the wall in front of the terrace facing the water. Waterside was then becoming built up with a continuous line of cottages on the left and a pair facing upstream beside a slope into the water connected with another near the mill where horses could refresh themselves or cool their tired hooves.

This 1910 view across the moor toward the houses of Waterside includes a large area of watercress beds excavated beside the natural course of the River Chess and irrigated by it. The semi-detached houses at the right edge are in Moor Road just along from the engineering works.

A closer look at Moor Road on a 1925 postcard includes the new terrace of Shantung Place, and, further left, the frame of the distant gas-holder. The water in the foreground is the overflow from the mill-pond, which slowly flows back to rejoin the true river. The overflow was later culverted from the controlling sluice by Kitty's Bridge, reappearing close to the road.

Pictured in 1910, Lower Moor, below Lord's Mill between the outflow from the mill and the old river in front of the houses of Bois Moor Road, became common property before 1900 when the Urban District Council bought the rights from Lord Chesham. They then started converting the marshy area into a recreation ground by burying the town's rubbish there to raise the surface level.

The Unicorn Hotel was planned as the Railway Hotel, situated by the intended terminus of the line. In the end the railway passed by on the other side of Bois Moor Road and the hotel simply became a 'local'. The river was diverted around the hotel but the town boundary still followed its original line, leaving the inn's front door in Chesham Bois and its back in Chesham.

This 1905 photograph of the part of Waterside then in Chesham Bois was taken from above the railway line near the entrance to Bois Wood. The line of Victorian houses in Bois Moor Road in the foreground, then the limit of the town's southerly development, included a general store serving the growing community on that side of the Moor. The heart of Waterside can be seen in the distant valley.

Watercress-growing, a flourishing Chesham industry by the 1850s, was given a double boost by the new railway. Gravel extraction for its construction created more lakes in which the cress could grow and the trains gave quick transport to the London market. Watercress beds near the Unicorn used water from the Chess, augmented by artesian wells like this, dug by Cheelds of Waterside Ironworks.

Pictured in 1900, these men were picking the watercress. Packed in wooden baskets it was then taken by train, mostly to Covent Garden market. At its peak the trade warranted special trains, but demand declined in the 1930s, though in the 1950s, the last days of steam on the line, waiting passengers still shared the platform with stacks of dripping baskets of cress.

By 1925 development extended further along Bois Moor Road with these semi-detached houses around the corner below the railway line. They are seen here across the mill-pond of Cannon Mill, the next after Lords Mill down the valley. The small building behind the telegraph pole is the 'Iron Mission', of St Leonards in Chesham Bois.

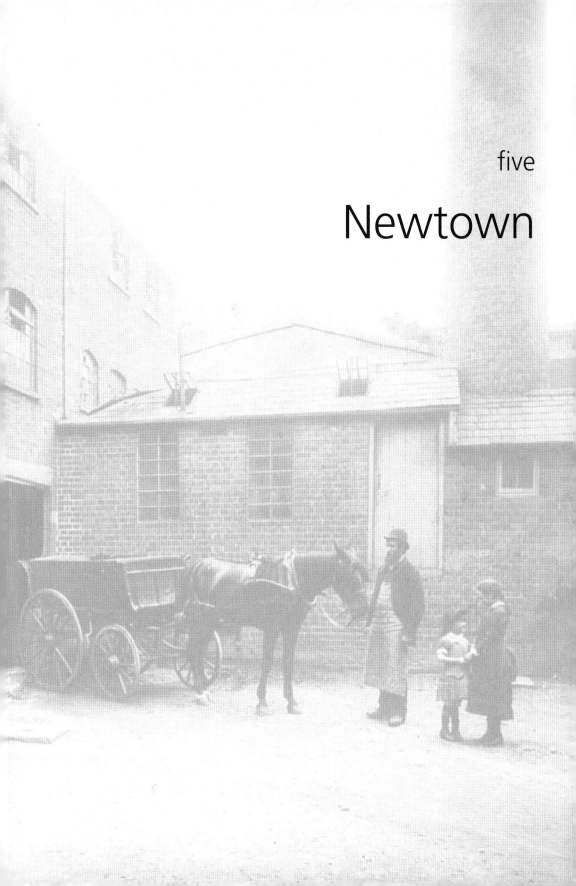

five

Newtown

The Revd Walter Wynn turning the sod of the Dell Meadow for the Chesham United Free Church.

S. Butts.

Above and opposite above: In 1906 the Revd Walter Wynn and many members of the General Baptist Church broke away and set up the Chesham United Free Church, also known as the United Methodist Church. The next year they built a new church on a plot just beyond the Friends Meeting House in Bellingdon Road, previously known as Quaker Lane. The first photograph shows the ceremonial start of the building work there and the second photograph shows the completed church. The congregation was badly hit by the 1930 slump in the boot industry and in 1933 the building was sold to the Chesham Methodists whose previous chapel had been in Broad Street next to the police station. The building then remained in use until dry rot and woodworm necessitated its replacement in 1965.

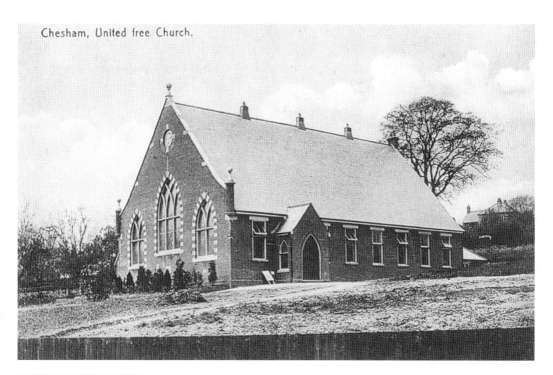

Chesham, United free Church.

When Frederick East started woodware manufacture in 1895, his was just one of twenty such firms in the town employing the craftsmen who had learned their skills in individual small workshops. This 1935 photograph shows his sawmill on the north side of Townsend Road with the usual pile of logs in the factory yard.

Also in Townsend Road, Robert Webb's new brush factory opened in 1890, a few years before the closure of their old works off Broadway. This early 1900s view is of the entrance beside the end house of a Victorian terrace in Townsend Road. At this date, the factory was able to take advantage of reduced coal prices, thanks to the railway.

Pictured in 1907 at the junction of Townsend Road and Broad Street, this was the first procession of the new Chesham United Free Church Sunday School. Offering an excuse to wear best clothes, such processions and the annual outing, often to Burnham Beeches, were the highlights of their calendar, and for some was the only reason for attending church during the rest of the year.

Opposite below: In another early view of Webb's works, a horse-drawn cart stands in the yard in front of the engine house which powered the machinery. Later amalgamated with another brush-maker, Webb's remained here for nearly 100 years, and was then replaced by a do-it-yourself warehouse.

This winter scene in Broad Street was captured by William Butts in 1895. The main building, Chesham's police station since the move from Church Street in 1861, was then staffed by Inspector Charles Summers, two sergeants and seven constables. In 1931 the station was rebuilt to incorporate the Petty Sessions court house.

The field next to the police station was filled with this terrace of houses in 1900. Photographer Sydney Jowett, who lived in the house marked with a cross, took this photograph in the 1930s, just after the British Legion Headquarters had been built beyond the terrace. The widening of part of the road, beyond the dustcart, gave rise to the name Broad Street.

Sydney Jowett, who was Chesham's main photographer from 1910 until the 1930s, took this photograph of a platoon of Northumberland Fusiliers on parade in Broad Street in the early days of the First World War from his upstairs window. Behind the troops, A.E. Gladden, a cycle dealer, repairer and maker of the 'Cestreham' cycle had just advanced into the repair of motorcycles.

Primarily a residential road, a few shops were scattered among the houses of Broad Street. Originally known only as part of Berkhampstead Road, it was renamed in 1901, but the continuous house numbering was retained. Pictured in the late 1920s, Mesdames Scott & East's milliners, ladies' and children's outfitters and fancy draper's shop was known as the Bon Marché.

Left and below: Beechwood's late Victorian brush factory was one of the largest in Chesham, extending from Higham Road through to Bellingdon Road with a timber yard on the other side of Higham Road on Higham Mead. In March 1930 the main building was destroyed by fire, an ever-present risk in these works, with their highly inflammable raw materials, wood, varnish and paints. In the upper photograph, the fire engine's escape ladder is raised and the yard is already awash with water. At its height the fire produced a pall of smoke which enveloped much of Newtown and in the second photograph the firemen are playing their hoses through the smoke into the ground floor, watched by many of the locals, probably worried that the fire would spread to their houses.

The following day firemen were still damping down the remaining pockets of fire in the burnt-out shell of the building, which looks superficially sound and was later rebuilt for many more years of service. (CTMP)

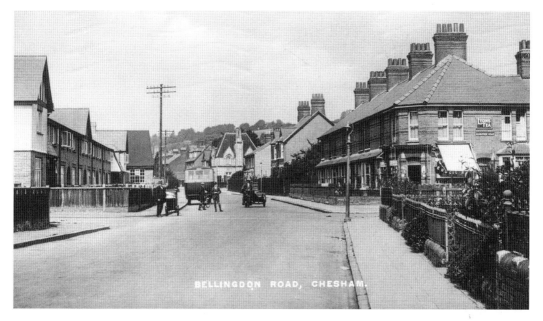

Past Beechwood's works in Bellingdon Road, the Sunnyside Road corner is pictured in the late 1920s, when the shop was Joseph Baker's grocery. The bus is standing by a newly built terrace and beyond it is the ornate building of Cemetery Lodge at the gate leading to the Anglican Chapel within; a matching lodge and gate in Berkamsted Road led to the Non-Conformist Chapel.

Timber merchant E. Fitzgerald operated a sawmill on a large site in Bellingdon Road opposite the Cemetery Lodge in about 1920. Here a traction engine is delivering a huge section of tree trunk to the yard from where a fully mechanised gantry would convey it into the mill. (CTMP)

Seen from the Berkhamsted Road end in 1910, the terraced Victorian houses of Sunnyside Road stretch away into the distance in a line broken only by an alley leading to Higham Mead. The houses on the right back onto the cemetery which had opened in 1858 and the three-storey factory at this end is squeezed into a wedge-shaped plot between Bellingdon road and the cemetery drive.

Eskdale Avenue, Chesham.

On the other side of Berkhamsted Road, Eskdale Avenue climbs the hillside. Development started in the 1890s through the garden of the Sportsman Inn, opposite Sunnyside Road. When photographed around 1910, it ended just around the first corner. Fifteen years later it was completed to Codmore Cross, the extension first named Khartoum Avenue, a title which was soon abandoned.

Above and below: Thomas Wright started making the typical Chesham range of woodware in Waterside in 1877, including hoops, spoons, fruit bowls, bread plates, police rattles, and shoe and nail brushes. Joined by his son, they moved in the 1900s to Newtown Mills in Berkhamsted Road, pictured above with the usual piles of raw material. In 1911 their products were listed as brushes, barn and malt shovels, cricket bats and stumps, and general turnery, and in the lower picture cricket bats are being made in a remarkably tidy workshop in the Newtown building. (CTMP)

One of Wright's specialities not listed in their advertisement was the production of polo balls but in this picture one of their skilled craftsmen is turning them from the raw wood. (CTMP)

Like many of Chesham's other woodware manufacturers, Wright's suffered a serious fire. In May 1907 part of their new Berkhamsted Road sawmill was destroyed and this photograph of the disaster includes firemen still hosing down piles of charred timber, wrecked machines and twisted corrugated iron panels.

Left: After the fire, the ruined part of the works was rebuilt. In this photograph from the site, looking over Berkhamsted Road to the corner of George Street, parts of the new walls and door frames were already in place although the old chimney was still standing. Here a couple of workmen are using a plank as a lever to topple the chimney in the right direction.

Below: Slightly further along Berkhamsted Road, the residential Essex Road, leading up to Brockhurst Road along the slope, was built in the 1900s, and Chesham Co-operative Society opened its Newtown branch on the corner conveniently placed for the area then under development, in a building which still bears the Co-op's wheatsheaf logo.

Beyond Berkhamsted Road where the main road turns up the steep hillside as Nashleigh Hill, Vale Road continues toward the head of the valley. At the start of Vale Road, the Nashleigh Arms, now commonly called simply 'The Nash', was built before the turn of the twentieth century and is pictured a decade later with a group of customers outside.

Vale Road, once known as Chesham Bottom, suffers badly from flooding when cloudbursts in the surrounding hills create fast-flowing streams down the slopes which converge there. Pictured in 1937, Brandon's furniture delivery van made waves as it ploughed through several inches of water covering the whole width of the road and pavements.

Returning to Bellingdon Road, this divides ½ mile from the town centre, one road following the Ashridge valley, and the other, Hivings Hill, pictured around 1920 climbing the ridge between it and Vale Road. The development of Pond Park started on this ridge in the 1930s, with further building at the extremity of the town in the '60s.

six

Some Chesham People

Chesham Fire Brigade was formed in 1840 with a team of volunteers and a hand-operated pump kept in a shed in Wey Lane and pulled, when needed, by brewery dray horses stabled in a field nearby. An entry in Harrod's *Directory of Buckinghamshire for 1876* notes that the fire engine was then kept at Water Lane, the key obtainable from Mr Arnott, a hairdresser of Market Square. Augmented by another horse-drawn engine with a steam driven pump, and managed from 1894 by the newly created Chesham Urban District Council, this pump remained in service, kept under the Market Hall, until the council bought their first motorised engine. The fire brigade captain from 1890 to 1910 was J.G. Stone, a tailor of Market Square, who worked with twelve men, all of whom are with the engine when it was photographed somewhere near the church. (CTMP)

Above and below: The first motorised fire engine, a solid-tyred Leyland with escape ladder, which entered service in 1923, was christened Norah after the wife of the current Chief Officer, builder Ralph Howard. A demonstration of the new engine's pumping power drenched many onlookers and left Broadway awash when its water jet reached into Upper High Street from the foot of Station Road. In the upper picture, Norah is standing in Amy Lane, with the CO in the driving seat. The lower photograph, taken in Eskdale Avenue in the 1930s, is of a second, pneumatic tyred Leyland, bearing the council's badge.

This posed group of Chesham postmen, some wearing seniority bars on their tunic pockets and one, probably a new recruit, without the uniform peaked cap, was pictured around 1895 when the post office, under postmistress Agnes Devereux, was in Market Square. As with many of his prints, this was hand signed by photographer William Butts, bottom right-hand corner.

Chesham Brass Band was formed in the 1880s and was an immediate success, in great demand for functions around the town. Pictured at an unknown location in 1907, by then it had become a Silver Band, under bandmaster William Greenwood, a professional music teacher. In the 1920s, the band gave regular Sunday concerts in the newly created circular garden in Lowndes Park.

Chesham Cricket Club started life in 1848 and for the first forty years played on the dry part of Higham Mead, moving then to their present ground off Amy Lane. In the early 1900s a regular fixture was against a team brought by Dr W.G. Grace who was a personal friend of the Chesham Captain, William Lowndes. This photograph includes all involved at Dr Grace's last visit in 1907.

Chesham United Football Club was created in 1919 by an amalgamation of former rivals, Chesham Town and Chesham Generals. Initially they shared the cricket club's ground, moving to an adjoining site in 1932. The new club was an immediate success with the pictured team winning five local championships under captain George Barnes in only their third season.

This anonymous group of Chesham folk in a two horse carriage was photographed in Market Square around 1910.

In 1902 companies of the Church Lads' Brigade were established at both Christ Church and St Mary's, 'to keep the lads out of mischief'. St Mary's band of fifes, bugles and drums led their regular church parades and took part in many other events. This 1928 photograph is described as a 'farewell group' with no clue as to who is leaving.

This studio photograph of an unidentified Chesham lady in Japanese costume is described on the back as, 'A Souvenir of the Chesham Carnival, Peace Day, 5 August 1919' and was addressed to 'Maisie with love from Mabel', one of whom was probably the carnival participant.

Above and below: The last four scenes, all photographed by William Butts in the Chesham area in the late 1890s or early 1900s, include unidentified local people taking part in their normal activities. The above picture, in a typical Chiltern farm field, shows a reaper pulled by a team of three horses while men with pitchforks wait to gather the crop into stooks. The lower picture is of target practice at a rifle range where the marksmen take aim from the comfort of blanket covered hay bales while an official beside the hut uses a telescope to scrutinise the distant target and the ladies look on from the safety of wooden chairs behind a rope barrier.

The upper picture is of more farmworkers, here with a one-horse cart bringing home an enormous and untidy load of hay and bracken. This card was posted in September 1907 with a message that the addressee would recognise the pictured lodge but with no further identification.

The last scene is one of Butts' less serious photographs, of around 1900, that needs no description.

Other local titles published by Tempus

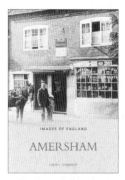

Amersham

COLIN J. SEABRIGHT

This collection of archive images, many never before published, highlights some of the important events that have occurred in the town in the last 150 years, such as the arrival of the railway in 1892. Aspects of everyday life are featured, from schools and churches, coaching inns and public houses, shops and businesses – such as Climpson & Sons' boot and shoe shop and Arthur Bailey's antique shop – to sporting events, leisure pursuits and local townspeople.
07524 3245 1

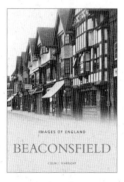

Beaconsfield

COLIN J. SEABRIGHT

Compiled from the author's own collection, this compilation of over 200 archive images includes vistas of well-known streets like London Road and Ledborough Lane, placed alongside images of shops, places of worship and schools. Pubs are also illustrated in this book, such as the oldest of Beaconsfield's historic inns, The Royal Saracen's Head, which is said to have been given the prefix 'Royal' by Richard Coeur-de-Lion in 1194. This is a detailed and informative volume.
07524 3093 9

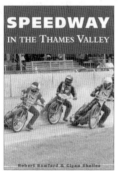

Speedway In The Thames Valley

ROBERT BAMFORD & GLYNN SHALLES

This in-depth account of speedway in the Thames Valley area details some of the aspects of the history of the sport, and looks at the variety of circuits used – from mountain-style tracks to oval circuits. Compiled by Robert Bamford, a prolific author of speedway titles, this book is an essential and enthralling read for anyone interested in either grass-track or speedway racing.
07524 2408 4

The Metropolitan Railway

DAVID BOWNES

The Metropolitan was the world's first underground railway. Opened in 1863, it presented a viable alternative to London's congested roads. By 1900 the network reached almost 50 miles into the countryside. It is probably best remembered for the creation of suburban 'Metro-land'. Spreading out from Willesden to Uxbridge, Watford and Chesham, the housing estates of Metro-land promised a modern home in semi-rural surroundings, well served by fast trains to the City
07524 3105 6

If you are interested in purchasing other books published by Tempus, or in case you have difficulty finding any Tempus books in your local bookshop, you can also place orders directly through our website
www.tempus-publishing.com